Because of you, I know what it means to love completely... you have taken me to a place I thought existed only in dreams.

Titles by Marci
Published by
Blue Mountain Arts®

Angels Are Everywhere!
Angels Bring a Message
of Hope Whenever It Is Needed

Friends Are Forever
A Gift of Inspirational Thoughts
to Thank You for Being
My Friend

10 Simple Things to Remember
An Inspiring Guide to
Understanding Life

To My Daughter
Love and Encouragement
to Carry with You on Your
Journey Through Life

To My Granddaughter
A Gift of Love and Wisdom
to Always Carry
in Your Heart

To My Mother
I Will Always Carry
Your Love in My Heart

To My Sister
A Gift of Love and Inspiration
to Thank You
for Being My Sister

To My Son
Love and Encouragement
to Carry with You on Your
Journey Through Life

You Are My "Once in a Lifetime"
I Will Always Love You

You Are My "Once in a Lifetime"

I Will Always Love You

Marci

Blue Mountain Press™
Boulder, Colorado

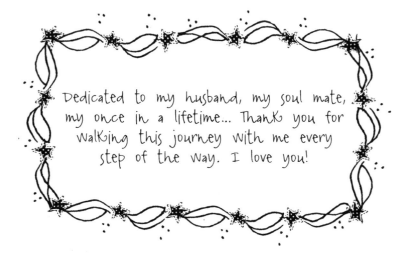

Dedicated to my husband, my soul mate, my once in a lifetime... Thank you for walking this journey with me every step of the way. I love you!

Library of Congress Control Number: 2011906562
ISBN: 978-1-68088-181-3 (previously ISBN: 978-1-59842-621-2)

Children of the Inner Light is a registered trademark. Used under license.
Certain trademarks are used under license.

Printed in China.
Second printing of this edition: 2019

♻ This book is printed on recycled paper.

This book is printed on paper that has been specially produced to be acid free (neutral pH) and contains no groundwood or unbleached pulp. It conforms with the requirements of the American National Standards Institute, Inc., so as to ensure that this book will last and be enjoyed by future generations.

Blue Mountain Arts, Inc.
P.O. Box 4549, Boulder, Colorado 80306

Contents

You Are My

"Once in a
Lifetime"

Once in a lifetime someone comes into our life that we really connect with heart to heart... soul to soul. A friendship develops and love follows.

With all of my being I know that you are my "once in a lifetime," and each time I think of you, I realize how lucky I am to have found you.

As time passes I realize just how blessed I am to have you as my partner. The journey of life, with its ups and downs, has made me appreciate the treasure in our love. The passing of time has given us a book of memories to hold dear. Thank you for bringing love into my life.

From the Moment We Met

I Knew We Were Soul Mates

That first moment when we met is etched in my heart forever. There was that sense that I have known you for a long time and that our relationship was meant to be. You have been there with me through the ups and downs, reminding me each day of why I love you. It is because of you that I know the bonds we form are as everlasting as the spirit.

Being "in love" is the best gift life has to offer... I have that gift because I have you! You stole my heart in a flash, and before I knew it, you showed me the real meaning of love. You showed me what it means to be loved for the real me... you showed me what commitment feels like... and you showed me how "in love" turns into "real love" through living every day with respect, caring, and the promise that we will be together forever.

Your Love

Is a Gift!

I can't remember when exactly
I fell in love with you. I cannot
remember a time you were not
a part of my life. You are my
companion, my helpmate, my friend.
Even though there are struggles —
ups and downs, joys and sorrows —
I know you are always there. The
commitment that you live brings
my greatest joy and allows me to
experience unconditional love.

Love Is

Love is the way you look at me.

Love is the way you call me just to say, "I love you."

Love is the hug that lets me know you are mine.

Love is the kiss that melts my heart.

Love is knowing that you are there when I need you.

Love is the way you miss me when I am gone.

Love is the way you give your best to "us."

Love is what you bring to my life each and every day!

Once in a while, if we are very lucky, we are in the right place to cross paths with someone special, and it's not long before we have that sense that a greater plan is at work. Love, trust, and mutual concern become the foundation of a beautiful relationship. With all my heart, I believe we were destined to meet. You were in just the right place, at just the right time, to make such a difference in my life... a difference that will last forever and one that I am so grateful for.

We Are Two
Hearts

Traveling in the
Same Direction

We have one of those rare connections that gives us such a beautiful relationship. So often you know my thoughts before I say them or sense what I need before I ask. Surely God's infinite plan has put you in my path... and selected you to be mine!

Love Is More Than a Feeling

I have grown to understand and accept that love is much more than a feeling. Love is an action. It is the way you show me each day how much you care. It is your gentle touch, your loving embrace, the thoughtful things you do. It is sharing together the good times and working through the tough times.

To love and be loved... that is life's greatest gift. To share that joy with you is a blessing.

We Were Made

for Each Other

If I searched the world, I could never find a better partner. You are a perfect example of loving and caring and compassion and concern. Just talking to you can make me feel better, and being with you reminds me of the most important things in life.

You Are Always
There for Me

...and I Am
Grateful

When I think of us, I realize that our relationship is one of the things I cherish the most in my life. It is hard to put into words how grateful I am for all the times you have come through for me... for all the times you have listened instead of telling me what to do... for all the times you have hugged away my troubles... for the laughs over nothing... for the many tears dried. Thank you for it all!

It is so good to have a partner who listens with a heart that understands my struggles... someone who knows the things I need to hear to put me back on the right path. God has blessed me with the good fortune to have you as my perfect match.

You Are Everything

to Me

You are a friend to me when I need a friend... You are a confidant when I need to unburden my worries... You are a mentor when I need to be shown the way... You are a bright light when I need a brighter day... In so many ways, you make my life so much better just by being you!

Because of you

Because of you, I know what it means to love completely... You have taken me to a place I thought existed only in dreams.

Because of you, I have someone to share the simple things... Your commitment to our life makes everything special.

Because of you, I have someone to share my dreams... The stars are within reach with you by my side.

Because of you, I wake each day knowing I am truly loved... There is no better gift in this world than that.

You Will Always Be

First in My Heart

Sometimes our stress-filled world takes so much of our energy that we neglect to let the person we love the most in the whole world know just how important they are. Because their love is always there, we can take for granted that it always will be there. I want to be sure you know that even though so many things take my attention, you are always first in my heart.

For all the times I forget to say "thanks" for all the little things you do... I want you to know that even when I do not say so, I am so thankful for your thoughtfulness, your caring, your willingness to please. Your efforts never go unnoticed.

Love

Love

For all the times I could have said the words "I love you," but they were not spoken, I want you to know that our relationship is important to me. Your love is a gift that I cherish and appreciate more every day.

The Angel in My Life...

Angels Are Everywhere

Is You!

Angels are at work in our lives every day... watching over us, prompting us to be compassionate, reminding us to pray, and sometimes working through others to bring an unexpected kindness that makes us stop and realize just how wonderful and giving the human spirit is! I feel so blessed because the angel in my life... is you.

I Carry Your
Love in My Heart

Always

Wherever I go... whatever I do...
I carry your love in my heart.
Your love becomes hope and makes
life's challenges bearable. Your love
becomes faith and inspires me to
do my best. Your love stays in
my heart each and every hour of
the day and reminds me that I
am not alone. I am so glad that
I have you in my life.

I Love You

and I Believe
in You

There have never been words
more powerful than
"I love you"...
or more meaningful than
"Thank you"...
or more sustaining than
"I believe in you."
So I'm saying these things to you now:
"I love you more than words can say.
I am so thankful for you.
And no matter what,
I will always believe in you!"

With You in My Life, I Have All I'll Ever Need

The way I feel when I am with you is one of those constant good things in my life. There is a sense of feeling understood... there is a sense of feeling loved and supported... and there is a deep sense of gratitude as I realize I have been given the wonderful gift of a kindred spirit.

You are always there with love,
encouragement, or a hug, and you
know exactly just what I need.
When I am down, you lift me up,
forgiving my mistakes and helping me
to forget them, too... When I need
encouragement, you let me know
that I am not alone... When I need
a hug, you wrap your arms around
me and tell me everything will be
okay... When there are good times,
we laugh and they are so much
better... and when we share sorrow,
it seems half as bad. I am glad that
you are in my life.

I'll Always Be Here for You...

No Matter What

I am always thinking of you...
believing in you... praying for you...
and hoping you know that no
matter how big a problem seems
or how hopeless you feel, you are
never alone, as my love is only
one hug away!

When You Need Encouragement, I'll Remind You of These Things...

You are stronger than you realize.

Life's inevitable adversities call forth our courage.

You have a lot of wisdom inside you.

God's plan will unfold with perfect timing.

The voice of your soul will lead the way.

I love you with all my heart!

One Day at a Time...

We'll Get Through
Life's challenges

It seems that life is always ready with a challenge just when we think everything is going along fine. Whatever comes along, please know that I will always be right by your side... When you are strong, you will have my admiration... When you are weak and afraid, I will hold your spirit in my heart and give you all the love I have... When you are overwhelmed with choices, I will be there to support the decisions that only you can make... When you have doubts, I will acknowledge them and remind you that God is with you every step of the way.

Our Love

Will Keep Us
Together

Our relationship means so much to me. If there are times we struggle to work things out, I will try to remember one thing... nothing is more important than our love. I know that love is the strongest force in the world, and with our joint commitment, we can get through anything.

There's Nothing We Can't Do...

Together

★

We may not have always understood the gift wrapped up in a greater plan. Time has taught us about the bond of love. We have learned together, sharing the good times and the bad, and no matter what, there has always been love.

★

★

It is not just "how I feel" when
I am with you, it is "who I am"
because of loving you. I am so much
more than I could ever be alone...
more joyful,
more alive,
more hopeful,
more positive about the future,
more comfortable with the past,
more sure of my purpose in this world...
and that is to remain forever
in love with you!

When we are very young, we begin to think about finding someone to spend our lives with. We imagine falling in love, and we believe that when we do, our lives will be complete. You are the one that fulfills that dream for me... You are the other half of my heart... and "falling" in love with you is the most exciting thing that has ever happened to me. "Being" in love with you each and every day is what completes me. You are my dream. You are my one and only.

I Want to Share Every Part of My Life With You

I want to share my life
with you...
every joy,
every sorrow,
every triumph,
every challenge,
every hope,
every dream,
every good thing
and every hard thing.

I know that our love will endure
the test of time and give to each
of us — separately and together —
the strength to overcome any obstacle
that comes our way. I will love you
forever and through all time.

I Think of You

Constantly

So many times I think of you, and I experience all over again the special times we have had. I remember a laugh we shared, and I smile. I remember our love, and I feel thankful. I think about how important you are to me in a world where everything else seems so uncertain, and I know I am truly blessed! A love like ours is a rare treasure.

We Have Been Given a Beautiful Gift...

the Gift of Each Other

We have each other... what a gift!
It is not often that a person comes
along who understands so much... who
cares so much... who gives so much...
who is so much fun to be with... who
forgives mistakes... who is always willing
to help... who is always there to listen.
Thank you for the things that you
give so freely and for being you!

You are the person who is there when I need to talk, and I know that you will be there sometimes to "just listen." You are the person that I can laugh with about the most important life events. You "know me," and that saves words sometimes.

I thought I knew all about life, but you taught me about a whole new world — a world where hopes and dreams were new... where love called me to be more than I ever thought I could be... and where I have experienced a connection that has allowed me to understand the purpose of life.

We Have Are Everlasting Bonds

I'm So Grateful

for us!

The most important thing I always want to say is "I love you." I am so thankful that we have each other and for the relationship that is "us." Your love and support are gifts in my life every day, and your friendship is something I rely on. I love you!

You've Made
Such a Difference
in My Life

For every day that you have loved me... for every time that you have told me so... for every look that lets me know what our love means... for the times you missed me, for the meals we shared, for the walks hand in hand, for the time spent in love, for every day that adds up to this day...

For the many kind words you have spoken... for the thoughtful things you have done... for the way you are always there sharing the special person you are... Thank you! You have made such a difference in my life.

You are everything to me, and when I look back, it seems as though my life began the day I met you. You stand behind me when I need support... You believe in me when I need inspiration... You love me through all times... You are the most important part of my life.

Where Has the Time Gone?

When I look back on our life together and wonder where the time has gone, I realize the road behind us is full of the gifts that make us rich:
hard-earned wisdom...
an appreciation for family...
trials that made us stronger...
hope given to others...
prayers answered...
love given and received.

The joys we have shared
and the memories we have
made through our lives are
a gift beyond measure.

Our Love Just

Gets Better
All the Time

When I first fell in love with you, I thought nothing could be better. But I have found that time has given us a richer and deeper love... a love that comes with a sense of pride and satisfaction. It's not just the good things we've shared that make our love what it is, but the rewards we get from navigating the obstacles in our journey and arriving at a stronger relationship. My life is so much more than I could have ever imagined because you are in it... You are the other half of my heart, my partner in life, and my best friend.

My Darling,
My Love...

I Hope You'll Always
Carry These Thoughts
With You

You are the person of my dreams...
Every dream I have ever had about
the person I wanted to spend my
life with includes you. All my needs,
all my wants, and all my desires are
wrapped up in you. I could never
ask for a more perfect love, a feeling
of being so complete, or a satisfaction
so total.

Let's Make a Promise To...

1. Hold hands, no matter how old we are.

2. Say "I love you" every day.

3. Write love notes for each other to find.

4. Forget mistakes.

5. Forgive words spoken too soon.

6. Plan time alone together.

7. Focus on the things we like about each other.

8. Not expect perfection.

9. Try to be the person of each other's dreams.

10. Support each other through life's challenges.

11. Say "thank you" often.

12. Send e-mails that say "I love you."

13. Take walks together.

14. Hug and kiss every day.

Thank You for All
That You Are...

and for Being
a Part of
My Life Each
and Every Day!

Thank you for...

Your thoughtfulness, your caring, and your ability to give me hope in every situation.

All that is uniquely you!

Being a special light in my life.

Letting me into your heart where I experience a special spirit that is as beautiful as what I see every time I look at you.

You are the light that shines in my life when I need inspiration...

Yours are the arms that hug me when I need consoling...

You are the person I rely on to listen when I just need to be heard...

You are the one who says the things I most need to hear...

I feel so blessed to have you in my life.

With Each
Passing Day...

I Love You More

As time passes I realize how blessed I am to have you as my partner. I can see how much you love me when you look at me, and I can feel that love with your embrace. The journey of life and the passing of time have made me appreciate the treasure in our love and all that you are to me.

Let's always remember to thank each other for the gift of our love. Some believe love means "happily ever after," but we know that is the end result of living "one day at a time." We will experience love and joy, sorrow and pain. Let's promise to enjoy the good times and step through the tough times, remembering that our lives have been brought together for a reason, and that is our spiritual growth. Let's rejoice in the endless possibilities to extend ourselves in love and commit to the task. Let's learn to experience unconditional love and give thanks for our everlasting bond.

♥ ♥ ♥

I Will Always

Love You

Your love is the most important thing in my life. I know I don't always tell you, but I want to remind you of how I feel. When I am with you, the past and the future lose all meaning, as the "present" with you is truly a gift. Thank you for all you are to my life... my love, my companion, my friend. I will always love you.

About Marci

Marci began her career by hand painting floral designs on clothing. No one was more surprised than she was when one day, in a single burst of inspiration and a completely new and different art style, her delightful characters sprang from her pen! "Their wild and crazy hair is a sign of strength," she thought, "and their crooked little smiles are endearing." She quickly identified the charming characters as Mother, Daughter, Sister, Father, Son, Friend, and so on until all the people and places in life were filled. Then, with her own loved ones in mind, she wrote a true and special sentiment to each one. This would be the beginning of a wonderful success story, which today still finds Marci writing each and every one of her verses in this same personal way.

Marci is a self-taught artist who has always enjoyed writing and art. She is thrilled to see how her delightful characters and universal messages of love have touched the hearts and lives of people everywhere. Her distinctive designs can also be found on Blue Mountain Arts greeting cards, calendars, bookmarks, and other gift items.

To learn more about Marci, look for Children of the Inner Light on Facebook or visit her website: WWW.MARCIonline.com.